The Unforgiving Servant

MATTHEW 18:23-35 FOR CHILDREN

Written by Janice Kramer

Illustrated by Sally Mathews

Concordia Publishing House

ARCH Books

The kindly old king was awake with the dawn.
"Today is the day," said the king with a yawn.

He popped out of bed, put his crown on his head,
and dressed himself quickly in robes of bright red.

He ran down the stairway as fast as he could and climbed on his throne made of monkeypod wood and sounded the gong. "Bring me muffins and tea! And send all my messengers in here to me!"

The messengers came. And the king sent them out with orders to ride through the kingdom and shout:

“Whoever owes debts to the king must repay!
Be at the palace by sundown today!”

Before long a crowd of eight hundred or more had gathered in front of the great palace door.

They swarmed up the stairway and filled up the hall
until there was no room to stand in at all!

From high on his throne the king watched
with a smile.
Beside him the treasurer sat in a pile
of books! There were books on the table and chair
and more on the floor stacked up high in the air!

"Now let us begin," said the king. So they did.
They brought forth a moneybox, opened the lid.

As people came forward to pay what they owed,
that huge, mighty moneybox soon overflowed.

Then up to the treasurer's table there came
one servant who scarcely could utter his name.
He trembled and said in a voice very low,
"I haven't the money to pay what I owe."

"WHAT?!" roared the treasurer. "Then you will find it's Law Thirty-three that we use on *your* kind! A law that says clearly," he ranted and raved, "that you and your family will be enslaved!"

The servant ran up to the kindly king's throne
and threw himself down on the floor with a moan.
"Oh, please, sir, I promise that *somehow* I'll pay!
But give me some time to discover a way!"

Just how many pieces of gold does he owe?"
he king asked the treasurer standing below.
TEN THOUSAND!" The treasurer's answer was loud.
TEN THOUSAND!" exclaimed everyone in the crowd.

The king raised his hand, and they quieted down.
"That *is* a great deal," said the king with a frown.
"But I shall use mercy. I hereby decree
your debt is forgiven, and you shall go free."

Oh, *thank* you, my king!" cried the servant with glee.
"I'll always remember your kindness to me!"
His heart was so happy he wanted to sing.
What a wonderful, merciful, kindly old king!

He ran from the palace with wings at his feet and almost bumped into a man on the street. "YOU!" cried the servant. His smile disappeared. He grabbed the poor man by the hair of his beard.

"You owe me some money! By heaven, I vow
you'll pay what you owe me and pay it *right now!*"
"Oh, please," cried the poor man, "I *promise* to pay.
Just give me some time to discover a way!"

"TIME!" laughed the servant with cunning and greed.
"In prison you'll have all the time that you need!"
So saying, he dragged the poor man off to jail
with *no* lawyer, *no* trial, *no* money for bail.

JAIL

The news traveled fast, to the servant's dismay,
for the kindly old king heard
what happened that day.

"*Find* him!" he ordered. "And bring him to me!"
The kindly old king was as mad as could be.

Just ten minutes later the sad servant stood before the great throne made of monkeypod wood. "Today," said the king, "I showed mercy to you. I canceled your debt. And then what did *you* do?

"You walked out of here, and the first man you met you threw into jail for not paying a debt! How shameful and wicked! Why couldn't you be as kindly as *I* was and let him go free?

"You don't deserve mercy!" The servant grew pale.
"I hereby command you be taken to jail!"
To prison he went for as long as he'd live,
the servant who couldn't forget and forgive.

DEAR PARENTS:

Jesus uses this interesting parable story to clarify His teaching about forgiveness.

In the preceding verses Peter asks, "Lord, how often shall my brother sin against me and I forgive him? As many as seven times?" Jesus says, "I do not say seven times but seventy times seven." One who knows God's unlimited forgiveness through the work of Jesus Christ will place no limits on his forgiveness toward others.

The parable, "The Unforgiving Servant," illustrates the point of such unlimited forgiveness. The amount of the servant's debt to the king is beyond imagination. He cannot pay the debt: all he can do is fall on his knees and plead for mercy. Out of pity the king forgives him the debt.

Now free, the servant meets a fellow servant and demands payment of 100 denarii, a tiny debt compared with his 100 million denarii. He refuses the poor man's cry for mercy and puts him in prison.

The king expected him to have mercy on his fellow servant. He now delivers him to the jailers.

Behind the king we see God. Behind the servant we see ourselves. We have heard the message that God has forgiven us our sins through the life, death, and resurrection of Jesus Christ. God still forgives us every day. His unlimited forgiveness makes us forgiving to others.

If we fail to forgive others, we can expect our heavenly Father to judge us as the king judged the unforgiving servant.

You and your child have received the forgiveness of God in the Gospel of Christ. Do you express a forgiving attitude to others in actions and words? Will you help your child live in the joy of God's forgiveness and lead him to forgive friends, family, and all people?

THE EDITOR